Why are there different Bible Translations?

by Michael Lane

evidence4faith.org

Why are there different Bible Translations?

Copyright © 2024 by Michael Lane

ISBN-13: 979-8-9909910-2-6

Evidence 4 Faith is a 501(c)(3) registered non-profit organization based in the United States of America. For more information on Evidence 4 Faith (E4F), visit evidence4faith.org on the web.

Some content (p.52) taken from The Interlinear Bible by Jay P. Green, Sr. Copyright © 1985. Used by permission of Hendrickson Rose Publishing Group, represented by Tyndale House Publishers. All rights reserved.

Scripture quotations marked:

Table of Contents

Introduction

Several years ago, I and my family were Christmas shopping at the Mall of America. I told my wife and girls that I was going to go to the bookstore while they shopped for clothing, and when they wanted to go for lunch, they could find me in that store. When I walked into the bookstore, I went over to my favorite place, the section on military history. I picked out an interesting book and started to read a section of it. Suddenly, I got a strange feeling and I strongly felt compelled to go to the Bible section of the store. So, I returned the book I was reading to the shelf and walked over to the Bibles. I soon found myself alone in a large aisle full of Bibles. As I stood in that empty aisle, I felt God wanted me here, but I could not figure out why. So, I asked God why I felt compelled to come and stand in this aisle in front of the Bibles? At that moment a clerk came walking down the aisle with two middle-aged ladies. They stopped within five feet of me, and the clerk said to the ladies with his arms raised, "Well, here's where we have our Bibles so go ahead and browse around. If you find something that is wrapped, go ahead and unwrap it. You can read it and put it back when you're done. Help yourselves because I must get back to the counter." One of the ladies stopped him from leaving and asked which one is the right one to use? The clerk turned with his hands up in the air telling them that he didn't know anything about them, so he left them standing there. The two ladies were looking at each other with frustrated and puzzled faces and then one said, "What are we supposed to do now?" The other said, "I wish someone was here who could help us." At this point I couldn't stay quiet anymore; and I said, "Excuse me, but I couldn't help overhearing your dilemma. Maybe I can help you." I asked them if they were looking for a specific type of Bible and they told me that they had just become born again Christians on Sunday and that they didn't own Bibles. They said they were told that studying the Bible is key to growing in their relationship with God, thus, they said they needed a Bible. One then asked me, "Do you know anything about them and what would be a good one for us to use?" I said actually I teach classes on this, and they were like, "Thank God for putting you right here!" So, for the next 90 minutes we proceeded to examine different Bibles as I explained how each translation was made, why it was made, what it was translated from, what its primary purposes are. They finally settled on one translation and they each gave me a hug. I gave them my business card and told them to contact me if they had further questions. They left me and headed for the counter to make their purchases with huge smiles on their faces.

It is amazing how often I am given opportunities to help people with translation questions. I recall one day back in the 1990s when I was teaching at a high school in Illinois and one of my students asked me a question towards the end of class. She pointed to my Bible I had on my desk and asked, "Michael, if the Bible is the Word of God, how come there are so many different versions of it?" On another day, not long after, a teacher and colleague of mine pointed to my Bible and asked me, "Michael, I know that you think that the Bible is the Word of God; but if it is the Word of God, why are there so many different versions of it?" Even recently, I was speaking at a women's retreat using a PowerPoint presentation on science and the Bible. As was usual for me, I was using various Bible translations of a passage, showing them how it was written in the English Standard Version, the New American Standard Version, New International Version and in Greek. During my talk, a hand shot up and I paused and asked the lady what her question was. She asked me, "Why are there so many different translations?" On another occasion just a few weeks ago I was speaking at a place and a person asked me what the best translation is to use. During this event, I had another person ask me which translation is actually the right one to use. Even on my last trip to Israel, one of my participants pulled me aside at a biblical place where we had read a passage of Scripture pertaining to it and asked my opinion on which translation he should be using to study his Bible.

Because there's so many different translations today and because of the frequency of these questions, I thought it best to make a simple booklet of the various popular translations. I have been teaching this subject to college students for almost 20 years, and we also have a podcast series about this on the Evidence 4 Faith website (www.evidence4faith.org, "Why are there different Bible Translations?").

This booklet is designed to help people gain a basic understanding of 20 different translations. We will examine:

- When each version was made
- What is the readability of each version
- What was the source of each version translated
- What was the purpose of making each version
- What unique features are found in each version
- What may be some pros and cons of using each version

There are different types or translations out there that can be broken down into four basic categories.

Formal Equivalency – sometimes called a word-for-word version. The scholars working to produce this type of version tried to maintain the words from the ancient manuscripts of Hebrew, Greek, and Aramaic languages. In other words, what they did was to examine the ancient manuscripts which they literally studied word by word trying to figure out what was the closest English equivalent pertaining to the meaning of the text.

Dynamic Equivalency – sometimes called a thought-for-thought version. For these versions, scholars chose to take sentences or even paragraphs from the ancient manuscripts and try to interpret what God was saying in today's modern language. In other words, they try to get the meaning across more than focusing on each individual word. These versions tend to be easier to understand, but they do at times contain paraphrasing of sections of manuscripts by the scholars.

Optimum Equivalency – is a combination of Formal and Dynamic Equivalency. Generally, they try to maintain a formal approach, but at times this becomes too hard to understand so they switch to a dynamic approach. In most cases, the reader is not informed when this happens.

Paraphrase – a work primarily of one pastor, layman, or scholar who takes a translation and rewrites it in his own words. As one would expect, the bias and theology of the one doing the work obviously stands out in these versions. The reader is subjected to the idea of what Scripture states according to the author. These are not that accurate, but they are often very easy to understand because they are written with a lower readability level. In some cases, the goal of the pastor or layman was to make a copy of the Bible in a very easy to read format for younger people or those not as literate as others.

My hope is that you will find a Bible that will help you grow spiritually in your walk with God. (Most Bible scholars suggest using multiple translations when you are doing a Bible study.) Also, that you will grow in your faith. What you are reading has been passed down through centuries and remains, almost miraculously, accurate.

Podcast Link

Follow along with the podcast version
at *evidence4faith.org*!

The King James Version

or the Authorized Version.

PUBLISHED **1611 A.D.**   READABILITY **GRADE 12**   TYPE **FORMAL**

"For the grace of God that bringeth salvation hath appeared to all men, Teaching us that, denying ungodliness and worldly lusts, we should live soberly, righteously, and godly, in this present world; Looking for that blessed hope, and the glorious appearing of the great God and our Saviour Jesus Christ;"
Titus 2:11-13 (KJV)

"The LORD is my shepherd; I shall not want. He maketh me to lie down in green pastures: he leadeth me beside the still waters. He restoreth my soul: he leadeth me in the paths of righteousness for his name's sake. Yea, though I walk through the valley of the shadow of death, I will fear no evil: for thou art with me; thy rod and thy staff they comfort me. Thou preparest a table before me in the presence of mine enemies: thou anointest my head with oil; my cup runneth over. Surely goodness and mercy shall follow me all the days of my life: and I will dwell in the house of the LORD for ever." **Psalm 23 (KJV)**

TYPE OF TRANSLATION: Formal. Considered a word-for-word translation, though the wording used is 17th century English.

PURPOSE: Authorized by King James I of England to be a version of the scriptures for the common man to read. Up until this time, most Bibles were the work of one or two individuals. King James authorized six committees totaling 47 scholars to complete this version.

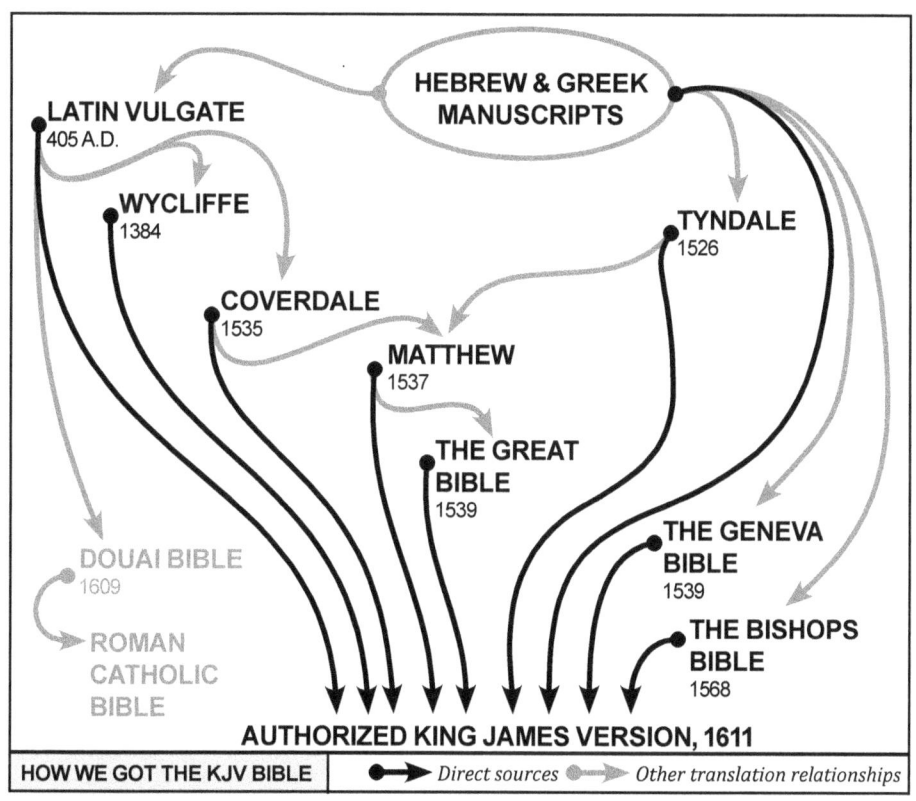

HOW WE GOT THE KJV BIBLE | ●➤ *Direct sources* ●➤ *Other translation relationships*

Chart labels:
- HEBREW & GREEK MANUSCRIPTS
- LATIN VULGATE 405 A.D.
- WYCLIFFE 1384
- TYNDALE 1526
- COVERDALE 1535
- MATTHEW 1537
- THE GREAT BIBLE 1539
- DOUAI BIBLE 1609
- ROMAN CATHOLIC BIBLE
- THE GENEVA BIBLE 1539
- THE BISHOPS BIBLE 1568
- AUTHORIZED KING JAMES VERSION, 1611

TRANSLATION SOURCES: Many previous bibles and ancient manuscripts. See chart.

UNIQUE FEATURES: It was written in a beautiful, flowing language that reminds one of Shakespeare.

PROBLEMS: No longer a common language. Difficult to understand. Words have different meanings today.

ADDITIONAL COMMENTS: Some people believe that the KJV is the only accurate version and the most accurate version to use. Even so, there are many mistakes in it due to changes in word meanings. It has been and still is one of the best-selling Bibles available. Many pastors and Bible teachers still utilize the KJV for a comparison text. It is also extremely helpful when using a Strong's Concordance or looking up words in their original languages in dictionaries because the universal Strong's Numbers are based upon this version.

The New King James Version

PUBLISHED **1982**   READABILITY **GRADE 9**   TYPE **FORMAL**

"For the grace of God that brings salvation has appeared to all men, teaching us that, denying ungodliness and worldly lusts, we should live soberly, righteously, and godly in the present age, looking for the blessed hope and glorious appearing of our great God and Savior Jesus Christ," **Titus 2:11-13 (NKJV)**

"The Lord is my shepherd; I shall not want. He makes me to lie down in green pastures; He leads me beside the still waters. He restores my soul; He leads me in the paths of righteousness For His name's sake.

Yea, though I walk through the valley of the shadow of death, I will fear no evil; For You are with me; Your rod and Your staff, they comfort me.

You prepare a table before me in the presence of my enemies; You anoint my head with oil; My cup runs over. Surely goodness and mercy shall follow me All the days of my life; And I will dwell in the house of the Lord Forever." **Psalm 23 (NKJV)**

TYPE OF TRANSLATION: Formal. Mostly considered a word-for-word translation, but at times leans more to a thought for thought or dynamic approach. Some consider it to be an Optimum translation, which is a cross between formal and dynamic. It has been endorsed by many respected Bible scholars today.

PURPOSE: To make a more readable and modern language version of the KJV.

TRANSLATION SOURCES: Unlike its predecessor the KJV, the NKJV is published by Thomas Nelson Publishers and employed 130 respected Bible scholars, church leaders, and others to use other scholarly versions and ancient manuscripts for clarity, including the Dead Sea Scrolls. They strongly utilized the Alexandrian Manuscripts while not utilizing the Textus Receptus manuscripts. This seven-year project included updating the vocabulary and grammar of the King James Version while preserving the classic style of the 1611 version.

UNIQUE FEATURES: It conforms to the thought flow of the 1611 version and is very much like reading the older version in modern English, which was their goal.

The Shakespearean wording is dissolved and replaced with modern language. For example, they replaced pronouns and verb form, including sentence structure, with modern English.

PROBLEMS: Even though its writers used other versions and ancient manuscripts, they chose to try to follow the KJV closely. Even so, some words and terms, not at all from Old English, have been eliminated from the text. This has caused some Christians to slight this version. Certain basic terms have been used less, such as "blood," "Jehovah," "soul," etc. In substituting terms and phrases, the NKJV sometimes uses terms that don't mean the same as in the King James Bible. Also, to some theologians, relying mainly on the Alexandrian Manuscripts instead of the Textus Receptus Manuscripts (the KJV used the Textus Receptus) makes this translation not on par with the original KJV.

ADDITIONAL COMMENTS: In spite of the few problems mentioned in the grammatical and word choice, and the main basis of ancient texts, the NKJV is considered by many theologians today as one of the more accurate and trusted versions of the Bible. I personally use it frequently and endorse it as an excellent Bible for studying.

The New Revised Standard Version

PUBLISHED **1989, 1997**   READABILITY **GRADE 11**   TYPE **FORMAL**

*"For the grace of God has appeared, bringing salvation to all ,
training us to renounce impiety and worldly passions, and in
the present age to live lives that are self-controlled, upright, and
godly, while we wait for the blessed hope and the manifestation
of the glory of our great God and Savior, Jesus Christ."*
Titus 2:11-13 (NRSV)

*"The Lord is my sheperd, I shall not want. He makes me lie down
in green pastures; he leads me beside still waters; he restores my
soul. He leads me in right paths for his name's sake.*

*Even though I walk through the darkest valley, I fear no evil; for
you are with me; your rod and your staff — they comfort me.*

*You prepare a table before me in the ppresence of my enemies;
you anoint my head with oil; my cup overflows. Surely goodness
and mercy shall folow me all the days of my life, and I shall
dwell in the house of the Lord my whole life long."*
Psalm 23 (NRSV)

TYPE OF TRANSLATION: Mostly formal. Often claimed to be a word-
for-word translation, and in most areas the text is. Some Bible and
university scholars claim that this is the most accurate English
translation available today.

PURPOSE: To make a good translation better. Scholars wanted to
make a new translation utilizing more manuscript evidence that

had become available. (The English language is evolving and is quite different from the 16th century era and has changed even in the 20th century.) Also, since the English keeps evolving, editors decided to include a gender neutral language in this new translation.

TRANSLATION SOURCES: A revision of an earlier attempt from 1952 called the Revised Standard Version, which was a revision of the American Standard Version of 1901, which was a revision of the King James Version.

UNIQUE FEATURES: This is a modern language version with gender-friendly pronouns. It is an accurate version. It was translated by a group of scholars including Protestant, Roman Catholic, and Eastern Orthodox Christians. For this reason, it is largely free of bias towards any one Christian tradition, though they made specific versions for Roman Catholics.

PROBLEMS: The wording of some Messianic prophecies is vague. For example: Isaiah 7:14 reads, "Look, the young woman is with child..." Instead of the more accurate, "Behold, a virgin shall conceive..."

They also made the controversial decision to translate some gender-specific words e.g., "people" in place of "mankind," "brothers" into "brothers and sisters." The fact that it is "gender inclusive" in some of its renderings prevented it from being adopted by most conservative and evangelical Christians.

ADDITIONAL COMMENTS: Though not popular among conservatives, it is none-the-less a good translation. It is endorsed by many in the Episcopal Church, the United Methodist Church, the Evangelical Lutheran Church in America, the Presbyterian Church, the United Church of Christ, and the Reformed Church in America.

There is a new NRSVue edition now available. (The "ue" stands for "updated edition.")

The Amplified Bible

PUBLISHED **1958, 1965, 1987, 2015**   READABILITY **GRADE 10**   TYPE **OPTIMAL**

"For the [remarkable, undeserved] grace of God that brings salvation has appeared to all men. It teaches us to reject ungodliness and worldly (immoral) desires, and to live sensible, upright, and godly lives [with a purpose that reflect spiritual maturity] in this present age, awaiting and confidently expecting the [fulfillment of our] blessed hope and the glorious appearing of our great God and Savior, Christ Jesus,"
Titus 2:11-13 (AMP)

"The LORD is my Shepherd [to feed, to guide and to shield me], I shall not want. He lets me lie down in green pastures; He leads me beside the still and quiet waters. He refreshes and restores my soul (life); He leads me in the paths of righteousness for His name's sake.

Even though I walk through the [sunless] valley of the shadow of death, I fear no evil, for You are with me; Your rod [to protect] and Your staff [to guide], they comfort and console me. You prepare a table before me in the presence of my enemies. You have anointed and refreshed my head with oil; My cup overflows. Surely goodness and mercy and unfailing love shall follow me all the days of my life, And I shall dwell forever [throughout all my days] in the house and in the presence of the LORD." **Psalm 23 (AMP)**

TYPE OF TRANSLATION: Optimal, meaning it is a combination of a formal or word-for-word and a dynamic or thought-for-thought translation. In my opinion it does lean more on the formal side of the spectrum.

PURPOSE: Scholars tried to instill the meaning of the words in the Bible, so they chose to include definitions and synonyms of certain words and phrases right in the text. They did this by adding brackets and parentheses. This of course makes some of the verses quite lengthy. In short, the translators did their utmost to "amplify" the words in the text to make them as clear as possible for the reader.

TRANSLATION SOURCES: Using the American Standard Version as their base, they also used available Hebrew and Greek manuscripts, including the Septuagint, Dead Sea Scrolls, and some of the best Hebrew and Greek lexicons available.

UNIQUE FEATURES: This version gives the reader the meaning and definition to selected words and phrases. It helps the reader to be able to understand the words of the Bible by giving synonyms or alternative expressions.

The chief leading figure of the groups of scholars was a woman, Frances E. Siewert. This was remarkable due to the social status of women in scholarly theological work in the mid 1960s during the birth of the Women's Movement. This fact alone, that a woman was a chief editor, has some churches and denominations refusing to acknowledge this translation.

PROBLEMS: The expressions and amplifications can be a hindrance, not all help. This means that some passages are extended in length.

Many of the amplifications can be subjective and opinionated by the translation team.

ADDITIONAL COMMENTS: The Amplified Bible is very unique and a different type of translation, unparalleled in both its development and style. It can yield insight of various terms or phases in the Bible, but these are not universally accepted or necessarily accurate. Therefore, though it is a good translation, I do not suggest it to be used as a sole study Bible but I highly recommend it as an excellent side source when studying a passage.

The New American Standard Bible

PUBLISHED **1971, 1977, 1995, 2020** READABILITY **COLLEGIATE** TYPE **FORMAL**

"For the grace of God has appeared, bringing salvation to all people, instructing us to deny ungodliness and worldly desires and to live sensibly, righteously, and in a godly manner in the present age, looking for the blessed hope and the appearing of the glory of our great God and Savior, Christ Jesus,"
Titus 2:11-13 (NASB)

"The LORD is my shepherd, I will not be in need. He lets me lie down in green pastures; He leads me beside quiet waters. He restores my soul; He guides me in the paths of righteousness For the sake of His name.

Even though I walk through the valley of the shadow of death, I fear no evil, for You are with me; Your rod and Your staff, they comfort me. You prepare a table before me in the presence of my enemies; You have anointed my head with oil; My cup overflows. Certainly goodness and faithfulness will follow me all the days of my life, And my dwelling will be in the house of the LORD forever." **Psalm 23 (NASB)**

TYPE OF TRANSLATION: This is a formal or a word-for-word translation of the Bible. The scholars working on this translation sought to make the most accurate Bible by translating the words in context from the old manuscripts. They developed a system to capture the word usage and sentence structures of the original languages.

PURPOSE: To make the most accurate translation by making it to be the closest to the original language.

TRANSLATION SOURCES: The Lockman Foundation had many conservative expert translators go back to the earliest Biblia Hebraica manuscripts, the Novum Testamentum Graeca, Dead Sea Scrolls, and other sources to do a word-for-word translation. They studied the original languages and the forms of those. They included paragraphs consistent with these manuscripts to establish context as well as meticulously choosing each word to match the original meaning. This removed bias from the translation, though it elevated its readability.

UNIQUE FEATURES: This translation was meticulously, thoroughly, and painstakingly put together following the grammar and terminology of the ancient languages in contemporary English. The scholars tried their best to find the true meaning of each word that God spoke.

This Bible is very unique in that the paragraphs in the oldest manuscripts have been included to help the reader know when a new chain of thought or thesis is beginning. They accomplish this by printing a bold face verse number or letter. Whenever a bold verse number is seen, it indicates the beginning of a new paragraph in the Biblia Hebraica. Archaeology has shown that the oldest scrolls existing today have the paragraphs in the same locations as the NASB. This helps one to follow the context.

PROBLEMS: This version is not as readable as some other versions but the NASB is one of the most accurate versions available.

ADDITIONAL COMMENTS: The NASB is one of the more difficult translations to read and comprehend, yet it is often considered one of the most accurate of the oldest manuscripts. Even sentence structure is not in the basic correct English used today. If you desire to study the scriptures in some of the truest meaning, the New American Standard Bible is perhaps one of the best Bibles available to the layman. It is highly recommended to use a NASB as a primary study Bible due to the fact of paragraph placement in helping the reader to determine context.

Legacy Standard Bible

PUBLISHED **2021**   READABILITY **COLLEGIATE**   TYPE **FORMAL**

"For the grace of God has appeared, bringing salvation to all men, instructing us that, denying ungodliness and worldly desires, we should live sensibly, righteously, and godly in the present age, looking for the blessed hope and the appearing of the glory of our great God and Savior, Jesus Christ,"
Titus 2:11-13 (LSB)

"Yahweh is my shepherd, I shall not want. He makes me lie down in green pastures; He leads me beside quiet waters. He restores my soul; He guides me in the paths of righteousness For His name's sake.

Even though I walk through the valley of the shadow of death, I fear no evil, for You are with me; Your rod and Your staff, they comfort me. You prepare a table before me in the presence of my enemies; You have anointed my head with oil; My cup overflows. Surely goodness and lovingkindness will pursue me all the days of my life, And I will dwell in the house of Yahweh forever." **Psalm 23 (LSB)**

TYPE OF TRANSLATION: This is a formal or a word-for-word translation. The scholars working on this translation sought to make the most accurate Bible after updating the New American Standard Bible in 2020.

PURPOSE: This Bible is not a totally new translation as it is an upgrade of the NASB. Like the NASB, scholars sought to develop a system to capture the word usage and sentence structures of the original languages. But it is slightly different from the NASB in format and terms.

TRANSLATION SOURCES: Translators used the NASB 1977 and the 1995 versions as a base for making this translation, but they also relied heavily upon the Biblia Hebracia, Novum Testamentum Graeca as well as other ancient sources. It was produced with approval of the Lockman Foundation (producers of the NASB), Three Sixteen Publishing, and the John MacArthur Charitable Trust. The work was done by the faculty of The Master's University and Seminary (where John MacArthur is the President and Chancellor) and reviewed by 70 consisting of a team of international scholars and pastors.

UNIQUE FEATURES: This translation was meticulously, thoroughly, and painstakingly put together following the grammar and terminology of the ancient languages in contemporary English. The LSB seeks to adopt words from the original languages of Hebrew, Aramaic, and Greek and say the same thing in English.

Translators decided to be precise in certain areas. Most notable examples include the use of Yahweh for God's name in the Old Testament, and the translation of doulos, the Greek term for "slave" (rather than "servant") in the New Testament.

PROBLEMS: Like the NASB, the LSB is not as readable as some other versions. Yet, it follows the words of the oldest manuscripts so carefully that it is a very accurate version. Also, because the LSB was composed by scholars associated with John MacArthur and The Master's University and Seminary, some pastors and leaders do not accept this translation as acceptable with other denominations.

ADDITIONAL COMMENTS: No doubt the greatest asset of the LSB is its precision to embrace the wording and grammar of the ancient languages, but this results in making the LSB not as smooth and fluid as other translations. Foregoing this, the LSB is an excellent translation and is worthy of being used as a sole translation for personal study. It is trustworthy to the ancient texts. Many serious students of Scripture will find this translation an excellent Bible.

The New English Translation

PUBLISHED **1996, 2005, 2013, 2019**   READABILITY **GRADE 8**   TYPE **FORMAL**

"For the grace of God has appeared, bringing salvation to all people. It trains us to reject godless ways and worldly desires and to live self-controlled, upright, and godly lives in the present age, as we wait for the happy fulfillment of our hope in the glorious appearing of our great God and Savior, Jesus Christ."
Titus 2:11-13 (NET)

"The Lord is my shepherd, I lack nothing. He takes me to lush pastures, he leads me to refreshing water. He restores my strength. He leads me down the right paths for the sake of his reputation. Even when I must walk through the darkest valley, I fear no danger, for you are with me; your rod and your staff reassure me. You prepare a feast before me in plain sight of my enemies. You refresh my head with oil; my cup is completely full. Surely your goodness and faithfulness will pursue me all my days, and I will live in the Lord's house for the rest of my life."
Psalm 23 (NET)

PURPOSE: To connect people to the Bible in the original languages in a way never before possible without years of study of Hebrew, Aramaic, and Greek. It is written in a dynamic (thought-for-thought) manner, but the study notes convey a formal (word-for-word) edition. Thus, they attempted to solve the problem between the two translations methods. Scholars disagree if it is either. It most likely fits closer to an optimal equivalence, but often is more dynamic in its reading.

TRANSLATION SOURCES: The translator used the best currently available Hebrew, Aramaic, and Greek texts including the Masoretic Text, Biblia Hebraica, Novum Testamentum Graece, and many others.

UNIQUE FEATURES: Beginning in the 1990s a multi-denominational team of 25 well known Bible scholars, experts in the ancient languages from various universities, produced this new version, first for internet and now in print. The text itself is primarily a dynamic or thought-for-thought translation, but the study notes are translated in a word-for-word format.

Over the years, hundreds of Bible scholars have made study note contributions to this translation, producing a version with 60,932 translators' notes! This is the most of any translation available today.

This Bible is easy to read and provides a plethora of notes on words, phrases, and history of texts that any pastor, missionary, or scholar will love. It is like having access to a hundred Bible scholars to help explain the Word, without having one denomination emphasizing its doctrine.

PROBLEMS: The text of the NET sometimes is a little too dynamic in its renderings, delving into interpretation rather than simply translating the ancient languages. It attempts to write the text in a modern English, but this can lead to some misinformation of the original message. That is where the study notes become so useful.

Another problem is that, though it was designed for the notes to add clarity, some of the notes are not helpful to the uneducated or layman. They are more for scholars and are not useful to some.

ADDITIONAL COMMENTS: This Bible is designed to help the reader understand. In the editor's own words, it is like having 20 Bible scholars looking over your shoulder as you study the verses.

The English Standard Version

PUBLISHED **2001, 2007, 2011, 2016**   READABILITY **GRADE 8**   TYPE **FORMAL**

"For the grace of God has appeared, bringing salvation for all people, training us to renounce ungodliness and worldly passions, and to live self-controlled, upright, and godly lives in the present age, waiting for our blessed hope, the appearing of the glory of our great God and Savior Jesus Christ,"
Titus 2:11-13 (ESV)

"The LORD is my shepherd; I shall not want. He makes me lie down in green pastures. He leads me beside still waters. He restores my soul. He leads me in paths of righteousness for his name's sake.

Even though I walk through the valley of the shadow of death, I will fear no evil, for you are with me; your rod and your staff, they comfort me.

You prepare a table before me in the presence of my enemies; you anoint my head with oil; my cup overflows. Surely goodness and mercy shall follow me all the days of my life, and I shall dwell in the house of the LORD forever." **Psalm 23 (ESV)**

TYPE OF TRANSLATION: Formal. The ESV is predominantly a word-for-word translation.

PURPOSE: To give the average readers the most readable of an accurate word-for-word translation.

TRANSLATION SOURCES: The ESV was created by taking the scholarly accepted Revised Standard Bible and revising it to make a low readability formal translation. Using it as a base, 14 primary scholars in addition to over 100 scholars from various denominations around the world studied as many ancient texts as possible and older versions to create this word-for-word translation. They used the Masoretic text, the Novum Testamentum Graeca, the Dead Sea Scrolls, and hundreds of other manuscripts, but relied heavily upon the original languages.

UNIQUE FEATURES: This version is one of the most readable of any word-for-word translation. It has a literary style that still conforms to much of the ancient languages, but with a lower reading level.

Scholars tried to follow the original scriptures as closely as possible yet retain an easy-to-read Bible. In doing so, they specifically maintained a nondenominational take on the Scriptures allowing the reader to decide what God meant.

PROBLEMS: Some Arminian critics claim that the ESV is too Calvinistic in verses dealing with predestination even though the editorial team consisted of many various denominations, including Arminians and non-Protestants.

Even though it is made on a readability level of 8th grade, some adults still do not find the English grammar as flowing as dynamic translations or paraphrases. Grammatically, it is structured a little differently due to the editors trying to follow the formal way of translating. For some, its language does not resonate with all readers.

ADDITIONAL COMMENTS: The editorial team consisted of such scholars as J.I. Packer, Wayne Grudem, Alistair Begg, John Piper, R.C. Sproul, and others from various countries. The ESV is considered a very accurate translation. If you desire to study the scriptures in their truest meaning, the English Standard Version is an excellent source. Although some of the paragraph headings are not as accurate as the NASB, it does follow the oldest manuscripts in most points. Personally, I use the ESV frequently and it is one of my primary Bibles to study from. I often use it for speaking with high school students. It is one version I often recommend, especially the study Bible version.

The Christian Standard Bible

PUBLISHED **2017, 2020**　　　READABILITY **GRADE 7**　　　TYPE **OPTIMAL**

"For the grace of God has appeared, bringing salvation for all people, instructing us to deny godlessness and worldly lusts and to live in a sensible, righteous, and godly way in the present age, while we wait for the blessed hope, the appearing of the glory of our great God and Savior, Jesus Christ." **Titus 2:11-13 (CSB)**

"The Lord is my shepherd; I have what I need. He lets me lie down in green pastures; he leads me beside quiet waters He renews my life; he leads me along the right paths for his name's sake. Even when I go through the darkest valley, I fear no danger, for you are with me; your rod and your staff — they comfort me. You prepare a table before me in the presence of my enemies; you anoint my head with oil; my cup overflows. Only goodness and faithful love will pursue me all the days of my life, and I will dwell in the house of the Lord as long as I live."
Psalm 23 (CSB)

PURPOSE: To revise and update the Holman Christian Standard Bible of 2010 in an optimal equivalence (formal & dynamic) and make it more popular. They also wanted to remove the name Holman from its title, as it was a Baptist publishing company.

TRANSLATION SOURCES: Ten individuals served on the translation oversight committee. Added to this were about 130 scholars from 21 denominations. The translation oversight committee studied the

Nestle-Aland Novum Testamentum Graece, 28th edition, and the United Bible Societies' Greek New Testament, 5th edition. The text for the Old Testament is the Biblia Hebraica Stuttgartensia, 4th edition.

UNIQUE FEATURES: This version is a combination of a word-for-word translation and a thought-for-thought translation. They called this optimal equivalence. Editors tried to avoid being unnecessarily specific in passages where the original context did not exclude females in referring to gender. The translators tried to stay away from allowing personal bias of scripture. Editors tried to make the meaning of the original Word as clear as possible to the reader.

PROBLEMS: The CSB on occasion substitutes words from the original text to try to give a more modern meaning. This is mainly due to the desire to make this an optimal equivalent translation. This can lead to some bias as editors are trying to determine what God means in the text instead of relying upon the words themselves. This does make the translation more readable than a formal translation. Because over half of the Translation Oversight Committee were Baptists, this version is sometimes said to be a Baptist Bible. They did not utilize any Arminians such as Nazarenes, Pentecostals, etc.

ADDITIONAL COMMENTS: This Bible is an upgrade of the 2010 HCSB. After much review of the HCSB, the Translation Oversight Committee listened to the readers and made a few changes. The most noticeable was to change the use of Yahweh back to LORD. They changed the word tongues when used in reference to spiritual gifts to the word languages. They changed the use of the term slave to servant so not to offend people and to reduce the image of the history of slavery. They tried to be sensitive to genders in the use of pronouns so not to offend readers. The Translation Oversight Committee attempted to avoid any appearance of theological bias, but with over 60% of the committee being Baptists, this is hardly conclusive. Even so, some well-known evangelists such as Tony Evans and Alistair Begg have endorsed the CSB.

Phillips Translation of the New Testament

PUBLISHED **1958, 1963, 1972**	READABILITY **GRADE 10**	TYPE **PARAPHRASE**

For the grace of God, which can save every man, has now become known, and it teaches us to have no more to do with godlessness or the desires of this world but to live, here and now, responsible, honourable and God-fearing lives. And while we live this life we hope and wait for the glorious dénouement of the Great God and of Jesus Christ our saviour.
Titus 2:11-13 (Phillips)

TYPE OF TRANSLATION: The actual title of work is The New Testament in Modern English, which is a paraphrase and not a true translation. It follows a dynamic thought-for-thought methodology, but was not translated by a committee. Thus, it contains the doctrine of a single pastor. Though he attempted to do the same with the Old Testament, he died after producing just a few books of it.

PURPOSE: J.B. Phillips (1906-1982), a Greek scholar and minister in the Anglican Church in London, noticed that the youth in his church did not like reading the King James Bible, stating to him that it was too hard to understand. So, in 1941 Phillips began translating his Greek New Testament into modern English, complete with its London slang style. Because WWII was being fought, he was slow in finalizing his work.

TRANSLATION SOURCES: The New Testament in the Original Greek Westcott and Hort, 1881.

UNIQUE FEATURES: C. S. Lewis gave it high praise writing, "It is like looking at a familiar picture after it has been cleaned." Early versions did not contain any verse or chapter numbering systems and it was written in paragraph form. This made it hard to navigate. Later editions contain some numbers to help one find specific passages. Phillips chose to write the books as if he were the one actually writing the original book to give it a special feel. The text is written in the British style of English spelling.

PROBLEMS: Is not a true translation since it is the work of only one man. Some areas of the scriptures carry a personal bias as to their meaning. Phillips writes in the Introduction that he was not concerned about "minute accuracy" but rather wanted to convey the "vitality and radiant faith as well as the courage of the early church."

ADDITIONAL COMMENTS: Since Phillips was a highly respected Greek scholar, he claimed that his was a valid translation; but it is the work of one man, and cannot be considered anything more than a paraphrase. It cannot serve as a primary Bible since it is incomplete, though copies of some of his Old Testament books are available today in a book titled Four Prophets (Amos, Hosea, Micah, Isaiah). Despite this, Phillips New Testament is a good source if one wants Phillips' opinion on a verse from the Greek. It also has a definite British take in its reading. Overall, this is not a primary Bible to use for personal study, but it is a good side source.

The Message Bible

PUBLISHED **1998, 2002, 2018**   READABILITY **GRADE 4**   TYPE **PARAPHRASE**

"God's readiness to give and forgive is now public. Salvation's available for everyone! We're being shown how to turn our backs on a godless, indulgent life, and how to take on a God-filled, God-honoring life. This new life is starting right now, and is whetting our appetites for the glorious day when our great God and Savior, Jesus Christ, appears. He offered himself as a sacrifice to free us from a dark, rebellious life into this good, pure life, making us a people he can be proud of, energetic in goodness." **Titus 2:11-14 (MSG)**

"God, my shepherd! I don't need a thing. You have bedded me down in lush meadows, you find me quiet pools to drink from. True to your word, you let me catch my breath and send me in the right direction.

Even when the way goes through Death Valley, I'm not afraid when you walk at my side. Your trusty shepherd's crook makes me feel secure.

You serve me a six-course dinner right in front of my enemies. You revive my drooping head; my cup brims with blessing.

Your beauty and love chase after me every day of my life. I'm back home in the house of God for the rest of my life." **Psalm 23 (MSG)**

TYPE OF TRANSLATION: The Message contains the doctrine of a single pastor. It is a free paraphrase. It is the "Bible transcribed by a single pastor." It is a slanted version of the Bible in that the author wrote what he thought the Bible should say in modern English.

PURPOSE: To make a Bible that common people would want to read. The author states that he wrote it to "bring the New Testament to life for two different types of people: those who hadn't read the Bible because it seemed too distant and irrelevant and those who had read the Bible so much that it had become 'old hat.'"

TRANSLATION SOURCES: Written by Presbyterian Pastor Eugene H. Peterson by examining the Greek and Hebrew himself and rewriting them in a more modern and easier to read language. It reads like a novel.

UNIQUE FEATURES: Early versions did not contain any verse numbering system. This was to make the flow of thought easier to follow. It is written in paragraphs with the topic heading at the beginning of each topic. It is written in modern English with slang to make it more interesting. Many of Peterson's expositions and doctrines are quite readable and clear. Some passages are definitely misleading (such as 1 Corinthians 6:9-10 and many others.)

PROBLEMS: Peterson placed his own personal feelings and beliefs in the text. There is entirely too much interpretation. Not intended to replace the Bible. This is NOT a study or a primary use Bible.

ADDITIONAL COMMENTS: This is not a translation but a free paraphrase. It is the Word of God according to Peterson. Some of his comments are fine and acceptable, but others are definitely nonbiblical and even contrary to what is written in a formal translation. In other words, on occasion, Peterson distorts the Word of God. The main problem is how to know when he does this. Some have denounced this paraphrase as "evil" but I believe that is a bit strong. It is not meant to be a primary translation, but a supplemental source to use alongside good translations. If kept in that mindset, it can be useful. But I know many people who do not use it that way and utilize it as their primary study Bible. This can be dangerous. It can be useful at times, but it has great weaknesses.

The Living Bible

PUBLISHED **N.T. 1968, BIBLE 1971**   READABILITY **GRADE 6**   TYPE **PARAPHRASE**

"For the free gift of eternal salvation is now being offered to everyone; and along with this gift comes the realization that God wants us to turn from godless living and sinful pleasures and to live good, God-fearing lives day after day, looking forward to that wonderful time we've been expecting, when his glory shall be seen—the glory of our great God and Savior Jesus Christ." **Titus 2:11-13 (TLB)**

"Because the Lord is my Shepherd, I have everything I need! He lets me rest in the meadow grass and leads me beside the quiet streams. He gives me new strength. He helps me do what honors him the most. Even when walking through the dark valley of death I will not be afraid, for you are close beside me, guarding, guiding all the way. You provide delicious food for me in the presence of my enemies. You have welcomed me as your guest; blessings overflow! Your goodness and unfailing kindness shall be with me all of my life, and afterwards I will live with you forever in your home." **Psalm 23 (TLB)**

TYPE OF TRANSLATION: This is a paraphrase and not a translation. It is a thought-for-thought commentary containing the doctrine of a single individual. It is Kenneth Taylor's commentary on the Bible and thus, it is a slanted version of the Bible.

PURPOSE: In the 1960s, Kenneth Taylor wanted his kids and other teens to understand the Bible. He wrote the New Testament in books called Living Letters and then the Living Bible in 1971.

TRANSLATION SOURCES: Taylor would read to his children nightly from the KJV or the excellent RSV, but they seldom could answer questions about what was read. Working at Moody Bible and having to commute to work by train, he decided to write down the verses from the American Standard Version 1901 during his commute so his children would understand. He completed the New Testament books and called each volume Living Letters. It was well received not only by his children but by others. Billy Graham even promoted them. This caused Taylor to complete the entire Bible which he called The Living Bible. It instantly became a best seller.

UNIQUE FEATURES: The most unique feature of this paraphrase is that it is so easily readable.

A youth-oriented version was sold in paperback called The Way in 1972. This Bible was a first for it included sociopolitical commentaries and contemporary illustrations at the beginning of each book to appeal to its audience. A Catholic blue cover version was also made as well as a psychedelically colored cover for teens.

It was one of the bestselling Bibles when it appeared on the market.

It was marketed in various styles to appeal to people with a non-Christian world view.

PROBLEMS: This Bible is a paraphrase, not a translation, and evangelical youth embraced it. Taylor's own interpretations and theology of the Bible are exposed.

ADDITIONAL COMMENTS: It was the bestselling book in America in 1972-1974. Taylor had problems trying to get his work published. He finally formed a small publishing company in his basement to produce it. Today, Tyndale Publishing House is one of the largest Christian companies in existence. It is a definite paraphrase and is not considered to be a primary study Bible. If you want the opinion of Taylor and what he thought God was saying in a passage, you can read it in this paraphrase. This Bible was thoroughly attacked by mainstream Christian denominations when it was published, it was never intended to replace a good translation.

The New Living Translation

PUBLISHED	**1996, 2004, 2007, 2013, 2015**	READABILITY **GRADE 6**	TYPE **DYNAMIC**

"For the grace of God has been revealed, bringing salvation to all people. And we are instructed to turn from godless living and sinful pleasures. We should live in this evil world with wisdom, righteousness, and devotion to God, while we look forward with hope to that wonderful day when the glory of our great God and Savior, Jesus Christ, will be revealed."
Titus 2:11-13 (NLT)

"The LORD is my shepherd; I have all that I need. He lets me rest in green meadows; he leads me beside peaceful streams. He renews my strength. He guides me along right paths, bringing honor to his name. Even when I walk through the darkest valley, I will not be afraid, for you are close beside me. Your rod and your staff protect and comfort me. You prepare a feast for me in the presence of my enemies. You honor me by anointing my head with oil. My cup overflows with blessings. Surely your goodness and unfailing love will pursue me all the days of my life, and I will live in the house of the LORD forever."
Psalm 23 (NLT)

TYPE OF TRANSLATION: Dynamic. This is a thought-for-thought translation of the Bible.

PURPOSE: Due to the success of the popular paraphrase Living Bible, Tyndale Publishing wanted to make an easy to understand yet reliable translation of the Bible.

TRANSLATION SOURCES: The style of translation is dynamic or thought-for-thought. Ninety Bible scholars from various denominations used many selected versions of the Old Testament and ancient manuscripts including the Masoretic Texts, Septuagint, the Nestle-Aland New Testament, the Samaritan Pentateuch, the Dead Sea Scrolls and more. The 1996 version was deemed too biased and was revised by scholars to make it more accurate in 2004. Even so, the NLT remains on the far spectrum of the dynamic chart away from formal styles.

UNIQUE FEATURES: The most unique feature of this translation is that it is so easily readable. They have translated cultural terms into the modern equivalent. For example:

- Dates and time have been changed to our present calendar and clock.
- Monetary units have been changed to our currency.
- Measurements have been changed to the American equivalent.
- Metaphors have been expanded upon.

PROBLEMS: There is a great deal of hidden paraphrases in the passages. These can falsely give the reader a different meaning of many passages than what was intended. This is somewhat common in dynamic translations.

They try to get more into the meaning of words. This gives too much interpretation and not enough translation.

This is a thought-for-thought translation which required the translators and editors to try to "get into the minds" of the original authors. This methodology usually leads to bias.

Many passages have possibly lost their original intent due to taking a paragraph in the oldest texts and chopping them up into many paragraphs. This leads to lost context.

ADDITIONAL COMMENTS: This Bible has been endorsed by many excellent and popular evangelical ministers such as Charles Swindoll. It is an excellent translation for children and for people who are not necessarily searching for deep meaning in some sections. Because of the addition of paragraphs, it is difficult to establish deep meaning and intent in some passages. Also, it can lead to a loss of Jewish cultural understanding of passages. Yet, it is a solid translation for beginners or non-scholarly students of the Bible.

The Complete Jewish Bible

PUBLISHED **1998, 2016**   READABILITY **GRADE 10**   TYPE **DYNAMIC**

"For God's grace, which brings deliverance, has appeared to all people. It teaches us to renounce godlessness and worldly pleasures, and to live self-controlled, upright and godly lives now, in this age; while continuing to expect the blessed fulfillment of our certain hope, which is the appearing of the Sh'khinah of our great God and the appearing of our Deliverer, Yeshua the Messiah." **Titus 2:11-13 (CJB)**

"Adonai is my shepherd; I lack nothing. He has me lie down in grassy pastures, he leads me by quiet water, he restores my inner person. He guides me in right paths for the sake of his own name. Even if I pass through death-dark ravines, I will fear no disaster; for you are with me; your rod and staff reassure me.

You prepare a table for me, even as my enemies watch; you anoint my head with oil from an overflowing cup.

Goodness and grace will pursue me every day of my life; and I will live in the house of Adonai for years and years to come."
Psalm 23 (CJB)

TYPE OF TRANSLATION: This is something between a paraphrase and a translation. The author tried to follow the most reliable ancient texts and translate them exactly. Most scholars who accept it as a translation view it as a dynamic or thought-for-thought format.

PURPOSE: Dr. David Stern, one of the world's most notable Hebrew scholars and himself a Messianic Jew, wanted "to restore God's Word to its original Jewish context and culture as well as be in easily read modern English." Sterns states that he had three purposes in mind for producing this version:

To restore the unified Jewishness of the Bible, and, particularly, to show that the books of the New Covenant are Jewish through and through.

To express the Word of God – Tanakh and B'rit Hadashah together – in enjoyable modern English. To make it "accessible and easy to read, flowing easily from the page into the mind and heart, unimpeded as much as possible by the differences between the environment of the Bible and that of the present."

To make the CJB fully usable in a Messianic synagogue, where the B'rit Hadashah would be read in the service along with the Torah and the Prophets.

TRANSLATION SOURCES: It was translated from the Tanakh ("Old Testament") and the B'rit Hadashah ("New Testament"). Stern took the Tanakh from the Masoretic Text and for the New Testament he took the United Bible Societies' (UBS) The Greek New Testament, 3rd Edition. The B'rit Hadashah which was Greek, was restored to the original "Jewishness" of which the Letters were originally given. Stern also consulted "a number of English and Hebrew versions and commentaries" and because of this, some scholars deem this a translation and not a free paraphrase. Stern himself says it is "something between a translation and a paraphrase; since it is partly one and partly the other." He did have 28 scholarly contributors helping him.

UNIQUE FEATURES: This outstanding, scholarly work offers Bible readers a thorough, biblically Jewish version of God's Word. The names of the books are Jewish along with their English names (if different). Semitic names are used for people and places. It incorporates Hebrew and Yiddish expressions that Stern refers to as "Jewish English."

PROBLEMS: Though it is written by one of the world's leading Bible scholars and 28 contributors, it still is considered by some to be a paraphrase due mainly to the sole work of one translator. Because it was constructed by Dr. David Stern, some consider it a valid translation, but it does at times interpret instead of translate, which is often encountered with a dynamic format.

ADDITIONAL COMMENTS: Presenting the Word of God as a unified Jewish book, the CJB is a translation for Jews and non-Jews alike. It connects readers with the Jewishness of the Messiah. Names and key terms are returned to their original Hebrew and presented in easy-to-understand transliterations, enabling the reader to pronounce them the way Yeshua (Jesus) did. The CJB also includes a glossary of Hebrew words with pronunciation in English, Scripture readings for Shabbat and feasts and festivals, biographies of Rabbis and Sages, and many more study helps.

The New International Version

PUBLISHED **1978**
REVISED **1984, 2005, 2011**   READABILITY **GRADE 7**   TYPE **DYNAMIC**

"For the grace of God has appeared that offers salvation to all people. It teaches us to say "No" to ungodliness and worldly passions, and to live self-controlled, upright and godly lives in this present age, while we wait for the blessed hope—the appearing of the glory of our great God and Savior, Jesus Christ," **Titus 2:11-13 (NIV)**

"The Lord is my shepherd, I lack nothing. He makes me lie down in green pastures, he leads me beside quiet waters, he refreshes my soul. He guides me along the right paths for his name's sake. Even though I walk through the darkest valley, I will fear no evil, for you are with me; your rod and your staff, they comfort me.

You prepare a table before me in the presence of my enemies. You anoint my head with oil; my cup overflows. Surely your goodness and love will follow me all the days of my life, and I will dwell in the house of the Lord forever." **Psalm 23 (NIV)**

TYPE OF TRANSLATION: Dynamic. This is a thought-for-thought translation of the Bible.

PURPOSE: In 1955, a man named Howard Long began a ten-year quest to develop a new modern English translation. His goal was to give the public an accurate and clear translation of the Holy Scriptures.

In doing so these scholars would develop a translation through the eyes of the biblical writers, but it had to be readable by Christians and non-Christians alike.

TRANSLATION SOURCES: In 1965, over 100 international scholars from various denominations began to develop this new Bible. Instead of basing it upon an older translation, the committee worked from scratch with as many ancient manuscripts that were practical. In fact, up to this time few translations had used as many manuscripts or dissected them as carefully. In 1978, they published the first NIV. They also made a commitment to revise their work every few years due to the evolution of modern English. It was again revised in 1984 and was followed by a children's version, The New International Reader Version (NIRV) in 1996 and then the 2005 Today's New International Versions (TNIV) which included a more politically correct and gender-neutral text. This was very unpopular with evangelicals and was discontinued. The latest version came out in 2011.

UNIQUE FEATURES: This distinctive and very popular translation was developed by scholars from many different nations and denominations to make this a truly international version. Thus, it was hoped that theological bias would be non-existent, but being a dynamic format, it wasn't.

PROBLEMS: Since this is a dynamic translation there is some paraphrasing and bias, which removes some accuracy of the version. This makes it hard for the reader to know when the text is being paraphrased. This was somewhat corrected in the 1984 NIV Study Bible which includes many footnotes and commentaries on individual verses indicating when this happened.

To make this more readable, the translators took single paragraphs in the oldest manuscripts and chopped them into many paragraphs, thus making the intentional meaning confusing. This removes context and can mislead people into a false interpretation of meaning.

The newest editions have taken a political correctness and gender-neutral tones to become a more acceptable fit with modern culture.

The early edition such as 1984 is a better and more trusted edition than the newer revisions. The Study Bible of this edition was excellent.

ADDITIONAL COMMENTS: This is the most popular version of the Bible sold today, though the newer editions are less and less accurate. For instance, the newer versions are gender-neutral to people and sometimes God. Many evangelical denominations refuse to use the newer editions because of this. The older 1984 edition and particularly the NIV Study Bible is the better version, but it is no longer in print.

God's Word Translation

PUBLISHED **1995**   READABILITY **GRADE 5**   TYPE **OPTIMAL**

"After all, God's saving kindness has appeared for the benefit of all people. It trains us to avoid ungodly lives filled with worldly desires so that we can live self-controlled, moral, and godly lives in this present world. At the same time we can expect what we hope for-the appearance of the glory of our great God and Savior, Jesus Christ." **Titus 2:11-13 (GW)**

"The LORD is my shepherd. I am never in need. He makes me lie down in green pastures. He leads me beside peaceful waters. He renews my soul. He guides me along the paths of righteousness for the sake of his name. Even though I walk through the dark valley of death, because you are with me, I fear no harm. Your rod and your staff give me courage. You prepare a banquet for me while my enemies watch. You anoint my head with oil. My cup overflows. Certainly, goodness and mercy will stay close to me all the days of my life, and I will remain in the LORD's house for days without end." **Psalm 23 (GW)**

TYPE OF TRANSLATION: To give readers a new approach of the idea of Optimal Equivalence (formal & dynamic). They wanted accuracy, yet readability for even children.

PURPOSE: To produce an optimal translation of God's Word that would be written in the style of an American Literature book. It is designed to be in a single column with the exception of poetry, which would be in verse format as seen in literature books. They wished to make a Bible that the reader could truly hear God's voice in an easy-to-understand literature format.

TRANSLATION SOURCES: The translators based it upon Beck's New Testament in the Language of Today (1963) and a draft of his Old Testament that he just finished before his death in 1966. They were combined in one volume in 1976 with revisions and called An American Translation. In 1982, a committee began a revision, and several versions were made, until in 1995 the God's Word Translation was finally published by Baker Publishing. In making revisions, the committee used the Masoretic text and the Nestle-Aland New Testament for accuracy, which was also used in many of the other translations we have studied.

UNIQUE FEATURES: This is one of the easiest translations to read and understand because the sentence structure is designed to be short in length, allowing elementary children to be able to read and understand what it contains.

Written in a literature format, the English is very modern and flowing. The word usage often appeals to the reader. The publisher calls this natural equivalence meaning in a way that a native English speaker would have spoken or written like this if they lived in that time period.

PROBLEMS: Some critics claim that this translation is a "Lutheran" Bible because many of the translating board members were affiliated with the Lutheran Church–Missouri Synod (LCMS), the Society, even though it has no official ties to this specific Christian denomination. There are a few verbs that the translators used that are not the most accurate choice, but they did this for a dynamic approach to understanding. This means that the GWT does have ample paraphrasing in it. Yet at other times, if the passage or verses in the ancient texts were easy to understand, they utilized a formal methodology.

ADDITIONAL COMMENTS: The God's Word Translation is indeed an easy to read and understand optimal translation. Other translations may claim this, but the GWT delivers. It is an excellent choice for young readers, but it is also an excellent translation to use in Bible study. The GWT is endorsed by Billy Graham, James Kennedy, and Josh McDowell.

The Contemporary English Version

PUBLISHED **1995**   READABILITY **GRADE 4**   TYPE **DYNAMIC**

"God has shown us undeserved grace by coming to save all people. He taught us to give up our wicked ways and our worldly desires and to live decent and honest lives in this world. We are filled with hope, as we wait for the glorious return of our great God and Savior Jesus Christ." **Titus 2:11-13 (CEV)**

"You, LORD, are my shepherd. I will never be in need. You let me rest in fields of green grass. You lead me to streams of peaceful water, and you refresh my life.

You are true to your name, and you lead me along the right paths. I may walk through valleys as dark as death, but I won't be afraid. You are with me, and your shepherd's rod makes me feel safe.

You treat me to a feast, while my enemies watch. You honor me as your guest, and you fill my cup until it overflows. Your kindness and love will always be with me each day of my life, and I will live forever in your house, LORD." **Psalm 23 (CEV)**

TYPE OF TRANSLATION: The CEV is a dynamic or thought-for-thought translation. About 100 scholars and pastors worked to develop this translation. Thus, this is a valid translation and not a paraphrase as some claim. Even so, the dynamic is so extreme as the CEV is positioned from the far to the outermost range from a formal or word-for-word translation as one can be.

PURPOSE: In 1984 Bible scholar Barclay Newman focused his attention on how children read and hear English thus beginning the creation of a new translation for young children and those adults who struggle with English. In 1995, the Contemporary English Version was published using the United Bible Societies' Greek New Testament.

TRANSLATION SOURCES: The American Bible Society produced a popular Bible called the Good News for Modern Man New Testament in 1966 followed by a complete Bible, the Good News Translation (GNT) in 1976 with a readability of 7th grade. Then in the late 1980s through early 1990s scholars worked on a new version which would be on a low readability level that even people not associated with the Bible would be able to understand and comprehend. The Contemporary English Version was published using the United Bible Societies' Greek New Testament.

UNIQUE FEATURES: This is one of the easiest reading Bibles available today that is an actual translation. It can be read by people with little or no biblical background whatsoever, making it understandable for all people including adults that struggle with the English language.

It uses simple, positive words to explain certain meanings, such as for the word "adultery" found in most translations, the CEV's substitution is "being unfaithful in marriage."

The CEV uses gender-neutral language for humanity, but not for God.

PROBLEMS: The basic problem most have with this version is that it is so extreme in its dynamic approach that it contains a great deal of paraphrasing and bias. In other words, it goes far astray in some of its translating from what the actual words and meaning are. Some scholars consider it on the same level as the Living Bible or the Message. I believe that is stretching the facts too much.

ADDITIONAL COMMENTS: If you are searching for a Bible for very young children in grammar school, or if you struggle understanding modern English, this is a good choice. It does not follow the words from the oldest manuscripts, but it does try to make them understandable. Sentence structure is short and concise, making it great for an early reader.

The Berean Standard Bible

PUBLISHED **2016** (online) **2020** (hard copy) READABILITY **GRADE 8** TYPE **OPTIMAL**

"For the grace of God has appeared, bringing salvation to everyone. It instructs us to renounce ungodliness and worldly passions, and to live sensible, upright, and godly lives in the present age, as we await the blessed hope and glorious appearance of our great God and Savior Jesus Christ."
Titus 2:11-13 (BSB)

"The LORD is my shepherd; I shall not want. He makes me lie down in green pastures; He leads me beside quiet waters. He restores my soul; He guides me in the paths of righteousness for the sake of His name. Even though I walk through the valley of the shadow of death, I will fear no evil, for You are with me; Your rod and Your staff, they comfort me.

You prepare a table before me in the presence of my enemies. You anoint my head with oil; my cup overflows. Surely goodness and mercy will follow me all the days of my life, and I will dwell in the house of the LORD forever." **Psalm 23 (BSB)**

TYPE OF TRANSLATION: Optimal Equivalence

PURPOSE: To connect readers with the Greek and Hebrew root words and meanings in an easy-to-read format. Bible Hub wished to make a modern English translation, effective for public reading, memorization, and evangelism.

TRANSLATION SOURCES: Published by Bible Hub, the translation team was comprised of scholars from Bible Hub, the Discover Bible and several impressive experts who served on an advisory committee. Using as a base text the Berean Literal Bible (a formal translation) and the Berean Interlinear Bible, the BSB was created to offer an accurate translation of the Greek and Hebrew texts in a reader-friendly format. Its creators used a wide assortment of ancient manuscripts including the Masoretic Texts, the Nestle-Aland New Testament, Samaritan Pentateuch, Dead Sea Scrolls, and many others. It was an excellent source of manuscripts that they examined.

UNIQUE FEATURES: The BSB maintains the original gender designations in Scripture and strives to be as consistent as possible to the core meanings of the original sources. Accuracy was their goal.

It is not your average study Bible with extensive notes, charts, maps, etc. This Bible is one of a 4-tiered format. In other words, there are actually four different Bibles in what is labeled as the Berean Bible. They are the Berean Interlinear Bible (containing Greek and Hebrew texts) which is only available online, the Berean Literal Bible (designed to take the reader to the core of the Greek and Hebrew meanings) is a formal translation that is not available except online at present, the Berean Standard Bible (a modern English study translation, effective for public reading, memorization, and evangelism) and now available in book format, and the Berean Emphasized Bible (designed to bring out the full meaning and intensity of the original texts). As of now, only the BSB is available in hard copy. The Berean Standard Bible is also called the Berean Study Bible.

PROBLEMS: The main problem now is that though they are all available online in public domain, only the BSB is available in print. Many scholars who have examined it liken it to a more readable 1995 NASB.

ADDITIONAL COMMENTS: The Berean Standard Bible is a good option for those wanting deeper study, cross-references, and a reader-friendly format. Aside from the confusing name, the Berean Standard Bible is an excellent Bible. The translation seems to be readable and accurate, and I recommend it as a primary Bible for study and devotions.

The Good News Translation

PUBLISHED **1976, 1992**   READABILITY **GRADE 6**   TYPE **DYNAMIC**

*"For God has revealed his grace for the salvation of all people.
That grace instructs us to give up ungodly living and worldly
passions, and to live self-controlled, upright, and godly lives in
this world, as we wait for the blessed Day we hope for, when
the glory of our great God and Savior Jesus Christ will appear."*
Titus 2:11-13 (GNT)

*"The LORD is my shepherd; I have everything I need. He lets
me rest in fields of green grass and leads me to quiet pools of
fresh water. He gives me new strength. He guides me in the
right paths, as he has promised. Even if I go through the deepest
darkness, I will not be afraid, LORD, for you are with me. Your
shepherd's rod and staff protect me.*

*You prepare a banquet for me, where all my enemies can see me;
you welcome me as an honored guest and fill my cup to the brim.
I know that your goodness and love will be with me all my life;
and your house will be my home as long as I live."*
Psalm 23 (GNT)

TYPE OF TRANSLATION: Dynamic or thought-for-thought equivalence

PURPOSE: In 1966 the American Bible Society published a simple,
everyday English version of the New Testament. Encouraged by the
popularity of this, they proceeded to make an Old Testament version
as well, to form a complete Bible. They finished in 1976 and called
it Good News Bible. The name was soon changed to the Today's

English Version, which had its name changed to the Good News Translation. The goal was to produce an easy-to-read version of the Hebrew, Aramaic, and Greek texts that anyone, regardless of background could read.

TRANSLATION SOURCES: The seven translators used the Masoretic Biblia Hebraica Stuttgartensia for the Old Testament and the Greek New Testament published by the United Bible Societies 3rd edition for the New Testament. The chairman was a Southern Baptist named Dr. Robert G. Bratcher. Soon afterwards an Anglican, Catholic and an Orthodox version were made.

UNIQUE FEATURES: This is one of the easiest to read Bibles. When published, there were few English translations that were easy to read. This hit the market and its sales escalated to the point that as of now, over 244 million copies have been sold.

PROBLEMS: Because of the small number of scholars working on this translation and the use of only a small source of manuscripts, many pastors and colleagues regarded it as a glorified paraphrase and not a true translation. In some charts and books, it is listed as a paraphrase and not a true translation.

In making this easy to read, at times it is too dynamic and loses some of the intended meaning of the ancient texts. This is why some regard it as a glorified paraphrase and not a scholarly translation. In some verses, it does not conform with what God is actually saying and can lead the reader to false doctrines, especially concerning the Lord Jesus Christ.

ADDITIONAL COMMENTS: The GNT was a bestseller in the late 1970s. It was especially popular with teens. Endorsed by Billy Graham for use in his crusades, it was popular as well in the United Kingdom, and in 1991 it was the most popular Bible there. It was also used in making the film the Gospel of John in 2003. Because of the problems mentioned with this translation, I do not recommend this as a primary study Bible or one for personal devotion. There are much better versions out there for that. It can be used as a comparison Bible for reading, but bear in mind, it is not one of the most accurate versions.

The Interlinear Bible

PUBLISHED **O.T. 600 A.D** **N.T. 300 A.D.** READABILITY **SCHOLARLY** TYPE **FORMAL**

"Ἐπεφάνη (Has appeared) γὰρ (for) ἡ (the) χάρις (grace) τοῦ (-) Θεοῦ (of God), σωτήριος (bringing salvation) πᾶσιν (to all) ἀνθρώποις (men), παιδεύουσα (instructing) ἡμᾶς (us) ἵνα (that), ἀρνησάμενοι (having denied) τὴν (-) ἀσέβειαν (ungodliness) καὶ (and) τὰς (-) κοσμικὰς (worldly) ἐπιθυμίας (passions), σωφρόνως (discreetly) καὶ (and) δικαίως (righteously) καὶ (and) εὐσεβῶς (piously) ζήσωμεν (we should live) ἐν (in) τῷ (the) νῦν (present) αἰῶνι (age), προσδεχόμενοι (awaiting) τὴν (the) μακαρίαν (blessed) ἐλπίδα (hope) καὶ (and) ἐπιφάνειαν (the appearing) τῆς (of the) δόξης (glory) τοῦ (of the) μεγάλου (great) Θεοῦ (God) καὶ (and) Σωτῆρος (Savior) ἡμῶν (of us), Χριστοῦ (Christ) ↔ Ἰησοῦ (Jesus)," **Titus 2:11-13 (BIB)**

PSALM 23

PSALM 23

A Psalm of David.

¹Jehovah is my shepherd; I shall not want. ²He makes me lie down in green pastures; He leads me to restful waters; ³He restores my soul; He guides me in paths of righteousness for His name's sake. ⁴Yea, though I walk through the valley of the shadow of death, I will fear no evil; for You are with me; Your rod and Your staff, they comfort me. ⁵You prepare a table for me before my enemies; You anoint my head with oil; my cup runs over. ⁶Surely, goodness and mercy shall follow me all the days of my life; and I shall dwell in the house of Jehovah for as long as *my* days.

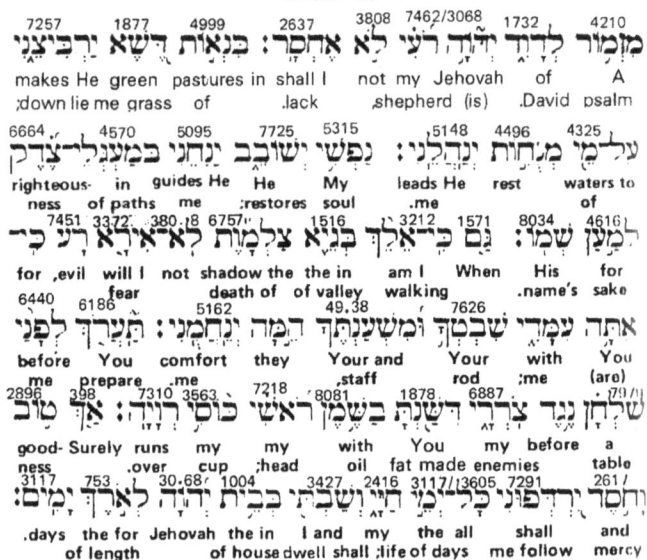

Psalm 23 photographed from *The Interlinear Bible Vol II* by Jay. P. Green, Sr. ©1985, Hendrickson Publishers.

WHAT IS AN INTERLINEAR BIBLE? An Interlinear Bible gives the ancient text on one line and, under it, the approximate English word for each Hebrew, Chaldean, and Greek word. If you simply read the English words, you are left, in most cases, with a confusing jumble of words. It is very literal but practically meaningless. As the translation becomes more readable in English, it will become less literal.

TYPE OF TRANSLATION: Formal. This is a word-for-word translation.

PURPOSE: To have the most accurate version of our Bible. This utilizes the most trusted codices in existence today.

TRANSLATION SOURCES: The Interlinear Bible uses the documented sources: Masoretic Texts, Nestle, SBL, and Nestle-Aland 28th Edition, Textus Receptus, Byzantine, Codex Sinaiticus and Codex Vaticanus, Greek Orthodox, Tischendorf, Westcott and Hort, as well as a variety of other manuscripts on which these critical texts are based. The Masoretic Text dates back to around 600 A.D. The New Testament dates back to around 300 A.D. These codices contain the oldest and most trusted word of God we have today. They retain the Hebrew, Chaldean, and Greek wording.

UNIQUE FEATURES: This is a copy of the oldest actual wording in existence. Since the original autographs are no longer among us, this the most accurate Bible available today.

Often, the original language words are accompanied by the Strong's Numbers or another word numbering system to help find the ancient words in a dictionary. These are extremely useful for additional study and reference.

Because it is called interlinear, the ancient text has the closest English equivalent along with the original language.

In some publications, the English equivalent words also appear in paragraph form beside the original language to aid the reader to understand what is written. Here is it being formatted to make it more easily understood. One may read these paragraphs and see the wording is a bit different with slight changes made to help the flow of understanding in English, otherwise the language is a hodge-podge of words that can be confusing.

PROBLEMS: The size of this work or the fact that it often appears in a multi-volume format, makes it difficult to work with. If it is in a single volume binding, the font is usually minuscule.

Though it is the original language, it is still not the original autograph for certain. Those scrolls and parchments have yet to be discovered if they still exist at all.

To be used properly, a basic knowledge of the ancient languages is helpful.

ADDITIONAL COMMENT: The term interlinear literally means written or printed between the lines of a text. This is in reference to the design of the translation. It usually has the ancient languages with the English words written between the lines. This Bible can be very useful when studying the ancient languages or attempting to learn them. Having the paragraphs in place allows one to know the context of verses, thus avoiding taking verses or passages out of context.

This version is considered the most accurate copy we have today of the original scrolls. Most Bibles are based upon these codices. All serious Bible students should make use of an interlinear Bible when conducting a word study method of interpreting scripture.

What's next?

Learn more about the Bible with free video and audio courses at *evidence4faith.org*!

BASICS OF CHRISTIAN LIVING: This 9-part course is focused on how to be a Christian and practice daily Christian living according to God's instructions through the Bible. This is a good starting point for new Christians and not-so-new Christians needing to learn foundational habits for a flourishing Christian walk. This course includes:

- How to do a Bible Study.
- Dealing with Past Sin.
- Is Church Necessary?
- What is God's view of Dating?
- What is God's view of Marriage?
- How should Christians live every day?
- What's with Offerings, Praise, & Worship?
- What is Prayer?
- How to listen to God?

BASICS OF APOLOGETICS: This 10-part course will help you understand the building blocks of your faith and be equipped to investigate the difficult questions about your beliefs. This series includes:

- What is the Bible?
- Why does the Bible have "Testaments"?
- Why should we care about the Old Testament?
- The New Testament is not just about love.
- The importance of Messianic Prophecies.
- The Old Testament on the Future.
- Is the Bible Reliable?
- How we got our modern Bible.
- Why are there four Gospels?
- How do I answer critics?